Martin Luther King, Jr. Day

I've got a fun activity for you on page 22!

M. C. Hall

Little World Holidays and Celebrations

ROURKE PUBLISHING

www.rourkepublishing.com

www.rourkepublishing.com

Photo credits: Mike Yoder/AP Images, cover, 3; David Quinn/AP Images,4; National Park Service, 5; Library of Congress, 1, 6, 7, 8, 10, 11; AP Images, 9; Shutterstock Images, 12, 13; Arvind Balaraman/Shutterstock Images, 14 ; Tomasz Szymanski/ Shutterstock Images, 15; Rick Rhay/iStockphoto, 16; Joy Brown/Shutterstock Images, 17; iStockphoto, 18; Jaime Duplass/ Shutterstock Images, 19; Christian Parley/AP Images, 20; Fotolia, 21

Editor: Holly Saari

Cover and page design: Kazuko Collins

Content Consultant: Keith Mayes, Assistant Professor, African American and African Studies, University of Minnesota

Library of Congress Cataloging-in-Publication Data

Hall, Margaret, 1947-
Martin Luther King, Jr. day / M.C. Hall.
    p. cm. -- (Little world holidays and celebrations)
Includes bibliographical references and index.
ISBN 978-1-61590-238-5 (hard cover) (alk. paper)
ISBN 978-1-61590-478-5 (soft cover)
1. Martin Luther King, Jr., Day--Juvenile literature. 2. King, Martin Luther, Jr., 1929-1968--Juvenile literature. I. Title.
E185.97.K5H254 2011
394.261--dc22
                            2010009913

Rourke Publishing
Printed in the United States of America, North Mankato, Minnesota
033010
033010LP

www.rourkepublishing.com - rourke@rourkepublishing.com
Post Office Box 643328 Vero Beach, Florida 32964

Why is this girl holding up this sign?

It is Martin Luther King, Jr. Day. It is time to **celebrate**!

4

Martin Luther King, Jr. was born on January 15, 1929, in Atlanta, Georgia.

When King was growing up, African Americans were often treated unfairly. Unfair treatment based on skin color is called **discrimination**. ★

The South had Jim Crow laws. The laws kept African Americans and whites **segregated**, or apart.

African Americans had to go to different schools from whites. African Americans had to eat in different places.

African Americans wanted to be treated equally.
They wanted to change the unfair laws.

King did not believe in fighting. He used **nonviolent** actions to change things. He made speeches and led marches to **protest** unfairness.

He asked Americans to work together. People started to listen to his ideas.

DAILY GAZ

April 4th, 1968 LATE EDITION

LUTHER KING

ASSASSINATE

CIVIL RIGHTS LEADER MARTIN LUTH

However, some people did not want African Americans to be treated equally. King's ideas made these people angry. In 1968, a man shot and killed King.

Many people continued King's work. Over time, laws were changed to give African Americans equal rights.

In 1983, **Congress** passed a law. It made the third Monday of each January a holiday to honor King and his work.

On Martin Luther King, Jr. Day, banks and post offices are closed. So are many schools.

Martin Luther King, Jr. Day has become a day of service.

People work together to fix old school buildings.

Other people fix meals for people who do not have money to buy food.

People clean up parks and other areas in a city.
These are projects King would have liked.

Towns and cities have parades to honor King.

People listen to songs and speeches about equality. King's ideas have come to life.

Craft: I Have a Dream

What you need:
- blue construction paper
- white construction paper
- scissors
- glue
- crayons or markers

1. King's most famous speech is the "I have a dream" speech. Write "I have a dream" on the top of the blue paper.

2. With an adult, cut cloud shapes out of the white paper. Glue them onto the blue paper.

3. Talk about your dreams. They can be for yourself or for the world. Write them on the white clouds.

4. Hang up the project so you can see your dreams each day.

Glossary

celebrate (SEL-uh-brate): to do something to mark a special occasion

Congress (KONG-griss): the group that makes laws for the United States

discrimination (diss-krim-uh-NAY-shuhn): treating people unfairly, sometimes based on skin color

nonviolent (non-VYE-uh-luhnt): not using physical force

protest (PROH-test): to speak or act against something

segregated (SEG-ruh-gay-ted): kept apart, often based on people's skin color

Websites to Visit

www.americanrhetoric.com/speeches/mlkihaveadream.htm

www.kidsforking.org/

www.mlkday.gov/

www.thekingcenter.org/PhotoVideo/Default.aspx

About the Author

M. C. Hall is a former elementary school teacher and an education consultant. As a freelance writer, she has authored teacher materials and more than 100 books for young readers. Hall lives and works in southeastern Massachusetts.